Milind D Zodge

Building Data Warehouse

This page intentionally left blank

Building Data Warehouse

Milind D. Zodge

Building Data Warehouse

DEDICATION

I would like to dedicate this book to my wife Deepa and my kids Aryan and Richa without their constant support I wouldn't have completed this book.

I would also like to dedicate this book to my parents for always guiding me.

This page intentionally left blank

TABLE OF CONTENTS

How to read this book

Every chapter starts with a summary of the topic covered in that chapter. You can review it and can decide to read it or skip it. This Summary is shown in this type of box.

Every chapter has key idea topics which are shown in the box like this

Each chapter starts with a high level view of the topic covered in the chapter. Mind maps like below have been used to display the big picture and focus area.

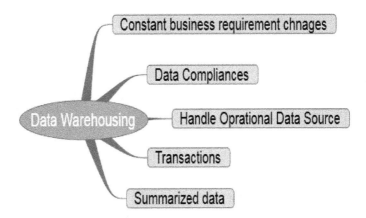

To illustrate the topic, practical examples are used they are shown by

INTRODUCTION

There are various books already written in data warehousing field, however my focus in this book is to provide a practical guidance on how the process starts after business strategy, how the information strategy and data governance implemented in data warehouse architecture.

I have tried to write this book in a different way to make it more entertaining to read which flashes key ideas. I have also added mind maps to layout the overall or big picture before starting the chapter.

Every chapter starts with the summary so you can quickly review it. Appendix covers lot of practical code and details of using PL/SQL.

Intended Audience

This book contains technical information about how to build data ware and PL/SQL code. It covers various sections of data warehousing like data capturing methods, job management and performance consideration.

This book should be helpful for data warehouse professionals of various roles from developers to managers, designers to architects.

Purpose of each Chapter

Chapter 1 has all the necessary terms of data warehousing. This Chapter is useful for any new DW professional to gain knowledge. If you are experienced in data warehousing you can skip this chapter.

Chapter 2 covers information strategy and its building blocks.

Chapter 3 covers data governance and its building blocks in data warehouse design.

Chapter 4 covers data staging strategy and its various options.

Chapter 5 Change data capture talks about some ways of capturing change data even if there is no standard way available. This chapter talks how to design to get change data captured.

Chapter 6 covers details of a new data warehouse approach.

Chapter 7 covers details on job management control information of the data load jobs.

Chapter 1

SOME BASICS

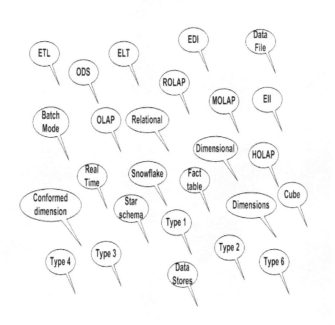

This chapter talks about all the jargons or terms of data warehousing. It sets the stage with industry definitions of these terms.

There are various data warehousing techniques to name some four E's; ETL, ELT, EII, EDI and there are few different methodologies or approaches like Life style approach, Corporate Factory approach or hybrid approach, there are star schemas, snowflakes schemas, stage, data mart, data warehouse environments, OLAP, ROLAP and MOLAP all these are discussed in this chapter.

Let us go through these jargons briefly so that we will have background painted.

Data Stores

Data stores are like a hanger for airplane. These can be used to store or hold data.

Data stores are of various types, like source data store, target data store, operation data store.

Source data stores can be used to store the data before transforming it. The structure of these stores is exactly same like source table with few additional control columns.

Target data store can be a data mart or table(s) of data mart while operational data store is a transactional, relational direct OLTP data.

Relational

Most of the source systems databases are relational in nature. By Relational I mean normalized database designed by following Cod's normalization rules.

Dimensional

Dimensional modeling uses fact and dimension tables. Data stored is in multi-dimension format.

You will have a fact table or your measures table in the center which will be joining to the required dimensions.

ODS

Operational Data Source, a transaction data which is operational in nature is stored in this data store.

Star Schema

It looks like a star as shown below.

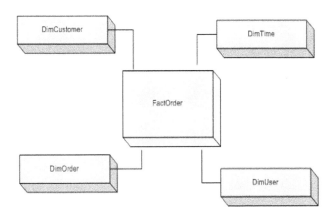

Figure 1.1 Star design

When you start extending your star schema it results into a snow flake

Snow flake

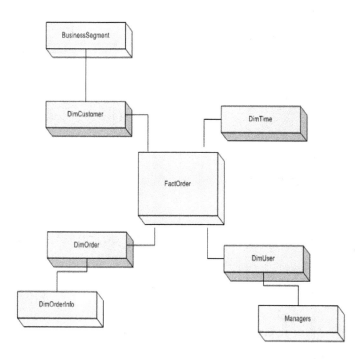

Figure 1.2 Snow flake design

Batch Mode

Batch mode, data is loaded in batch or in a timely fashion which is not real time.

Real Time Mode

Data is loaded at the same time or with very less delay.

Figure 1.3 4 E's

ETL

ETL, the well-known term for ETL is Extract Transform Load. It explains itself; extract to extract data from the data source, now data source can be a file, database, and message.

ELT

ELT, the well-known term for ELT is Extract Load Transform. This is similar to ETL the only difference is when the data is transformed. Both these techniques are usefully in a right place. Let us go through some practical examples of ETL and ELT.

Consider we have a SAP data source SAP has ABAP scripts which deliver files or tables. The desired data is pulled using these ABAP scripts and loaded into the data transfer tables. We want to read this data from SAP and push it to Stage environment. In this case you most likely want to have your stage table mimicking the source; I mean your column names will be same as of your source. So here you will use ELT, extract and load you will hardly do any transformation while loading the data. Now you want to move this stage data into your data mart or data warehouse now you will have to resolve all the dimension ids while loading fact which you will do it by transforming the data.

EDI

Next E is EDI; the well-known term is Electronic Data Interface. Let us see a practical use of this technique.

Let us assume you are capturing a detail of shipping data and want to have a real time feed of this data. Shipping department can send messages whenever shipping is done which can be stored in the stage tables. You can use this stage table as a queue to store messages which can be utilized by the ETL tool to take it further in the data warehouse.

EII

EII, our last E, stands for Electronic Information Integration, now what is that. It means a way to deliver the data based on business need. There will be a need in some cases to have real time data and in some cases hourly refresh is fine, EII basically represents all this different methods.

SMP Architecture

SMP symmetric multiprocessing is an architecture which focuses on share everything approach. What that means is you will have multiple processors for your application to use however all these processors shares the same operating system, memory (RAM) and the disk space.

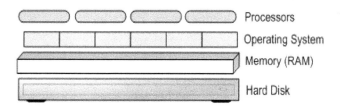

Figure 1.4 SMP architecture

The above diagram shows the different layers, not necessarily linked the way it is shown.

It is up-to the operating system to utilize the multiprocessor environment. You will have to build support for SMP into the operating system.

The application or program needs to be coded in such a way that it can utilize SMP for example using multithreading, multitasking. SMP is best if more than one program is running at the same time.

Some operating systems can even do a load balancing between these multiprocessor environments. This is mostly useful for operational systems or OLTP applications.

Conformed Dimension

If you are using bottom up/ Life Style/ Kimball's approach then you will come across this term. When you are designing data marts you will see many times using the same dimension in more than one fact table or across enterprise. E.g. customer, time, order, user

You can separate these dimensions and make them as a conformed dimension so that it can be used in all the other DW tables.

Advantage of Conformed Dimension: With the help of these dimensions you can join two or more separate fact tables which will result in joining both the dimension.

Type 1 dimension

If you are using bottom up/ Life Style/ Kimball's approach then you will come across this

term. Type 1 dimensions are just like regular OLTP tables. They do not preserve history.

Hence whenever there is changed data captured from the source, the target data will be inserted if the record does not exist and if the record exists, it will be updated with the new information directly.

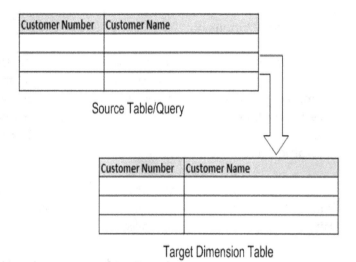

Customer Number	Customer Name

Source Table/Query

Customer Number	Customer Name

Target Dimension Table

Figure 1.5 Type 1 Dimension Table

Type 2 dimension

If you are using bottom up/ Life Style/ Kimball's approach then you will come across this term. Type 2 dimensions preserve history.

Hence whenever there is changed data captured from the source, the target data will be inserted if the record does not exist in target. If record exists in the target then the old record will be expired and new record will be inserted as an active record.

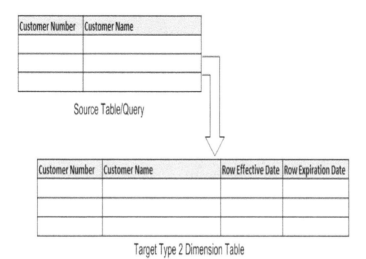

Figure 1.6 Type 2 Dimension Table

Type 3 Dimension

If you are using bottom up/ Life Style/ Kimball's approach then you will come across this term. Type 3 dimensions preserve history.

Hence whenever there is changed data captured from the source, the target data will be inserted if the record does not exist in target. If the record exists then the old record column will be copied to the old columns as indicated by the diagram and new data will be updated in the row column.

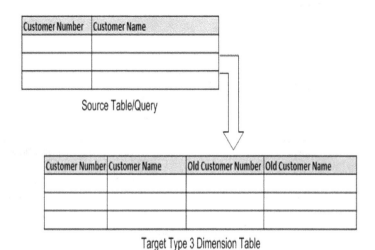

Source Table/Query

Target Type 3 Dimension Table

Figure 1.7 Type 3 Dimension Table

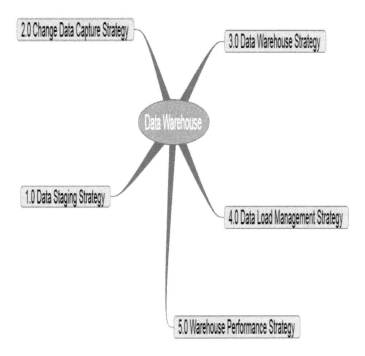

Figure 1.8 Mind map data warehouse strategy

There are five major areas you need to focus on:

1. Data Staging Strategy: Here you will focus how you want to store data in staging environment. There are various techniques you can consider while selecting the best suited for the requirement
2. Change Data Capture: Here you will focus on how you want to get the changed data on regular basis

3. Data Warehouse Strategy: Here you will focus on choosing a right data warehouse approach

4. Data Load Management Strategy: Here you need to focus on how you want to manage all the data load jobs and how you want to handle any job reversal in design

5. Warehouse Performance Strategy: Here you will focus on performance related design implementation you can do from the beginning

INFORMATION STRATEGY

In this chapter we will briefly go into details of building blocks of information strategy.

Any well-formed information strategy should have components like Situation Analysis, Business Capabilities, Conceptual Architecture, Information Architecture, Data Architecture, Current State Architecture, Future State Architecture, Technical Architecture and Roadmap.

This is the first stone of our data warehouse building.

Based on the business need Information Architecture is created aligning business strategy.

Let us go through each of these building blocks in some details.

Situation Analysis:

In situation analysis the focus is on analyzing the current situation. Analyze the business requirements from business strategy.

In this section we records current situation, Future State which align with business strategy and then what strategy/tools you will use to go to future state from current situation.

This is very important section in information strategy as it shows and forces you to align information strategy with business strategy. This will help you showing the business value of strategy.

Business Capabilities:

In business capabilities the focus is on analyzing the business requirement. Meeting with business and going through the business strategy meeting you can fill this section.

Record functional capability needs of business and process capability needs of business separately.

Conceptual Architecture:

Most of the time you present Information Strategy to non-technical person also, this is a very useful section for that.

In conceptual architecture you draw overall picture of information. Focus is given on the components like Source data/ OLAP systems, then Data warehouse, meta-data, information security and delivery.

Information Architecture:

Information Architecture is similar to conceptual architecture however this is in detail, which also has details on processes and/or tools used between each layer.

Data Architecture:

In data architecture focus is given on data flow and all the components used it in, like databases, file, document, tools, techniques, meta-data and outputs.

This is one of the technical sections of the information strategy document.

Technical Architecture:

In technical architecture focus is given on laying out the physical landscape. What servers you will be using, the communication protocol, repositories, database servers, web servers, https servers etc.

Current State Architecture:

This is preliminary data architecture in current state which shows data flow in the existing environment.

Future State Architecture:

This is preliminary data architecture for future state which shows how data will flow in target architecture based on the business needs.

Roadmap:

Roadmap defines the timeline factors and in general how strategy will be implemented. Take the defined strategy and define major activities needed to fulfill the strategy, note it down in this section along with the approximate timeline. This is not your regular project plan however the intention is to facilitate implementation of the strategy.

DATA GOVERNANCE

This chapter talks about how the six areas of Data Governance Program can be implemented in data warehouse architecture.

All these six area like Data Auditability, Data Accessibility, Data Availability, Data Quality, Data Consistency, and Data Security, are discussed briefly in the context of design of data warehouse.

Let us go through each of these building blocks in some details.

Data Auditability

Data Auditability focuses on how to audit track the data changes. Following can be done in data warehouse to have this feature in design:

1. To achieve this we will be adding created on date and modified on date for all the tables
2. Dimension tables have effective date and expiration date columns
3. Record DML reason code in the table which will use standard reason codes

Data Accessibility

Data Accessibility focuses on how the data of the data warehouse can be available for other applications to use it. Following can be done to have this feature in the data warehouse design:

1. A different schema can be created e.g. EDW_READ which will have all the required grants to select records from the tables. These will the only gateway to EDW for external systems.

Data Availability

Data Availability focuses on Data latency and when data will be available for reporting. Following can be done in data warehouse to have this feature in design:

1. Data will be available for reporting as soon as all the error is resolved or if there are no data loading errors. Data will be loaded frequently as per the need, daily, weekly, monthly, every 30 mins, every 15 mins etc.

Data Quality

Data Quality Focus on quality of data in data warehouse. Following can be done to have this in data warehouse design:

1. Data Quality checks
2. Balance and control checks will be performed to validate all the data is processed or not

Data Consistency

Data is validated with source in stage area to maintain data consistency.

Data Security

A security table can be created to handle the data security. This table will be used inside all the queries as well as frameworks.

This page intentionally left blank

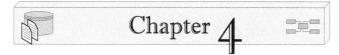

DATA STAGING STRATEGY

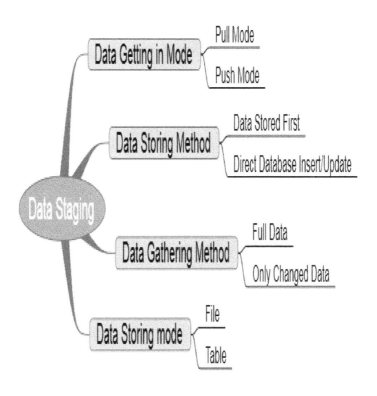

This chapter talks about different ways of designing data staging environment.

In data warehouse we have staging layer. Data from various sources is staged here temporary till it is processed and transformed into data warehouse.

There are various ways we can put data in staging layer. Like, pull mode, push mode. In pull mode data is pulled from the source and push mode is exactly opposite data is pushed into staging layer.

 Data in this layer can be relational in nature

Data Getting in Mode

Pull mode

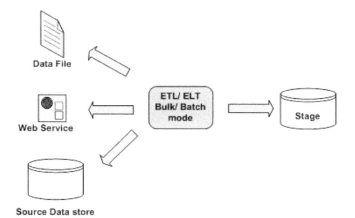

Data File

Web Service

ETL/ ELT Bulk/ Batch mode

Stage

Source Data store

Figure 4.1 Pull mode data flow for data staging

As the above diagram shows, data is pulled from various data sources by the ETL or ELT script and then stored in the staging layer.

Push mode

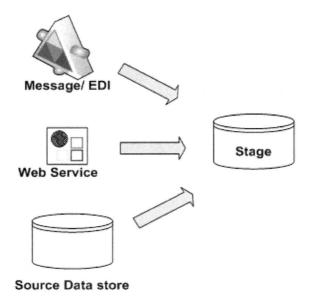

Source Data store

Figure 4.2 Push mode data flow for data staging

As the above diagram shows, data is pushed by various data sources and then stored in the staging layer.

Once you have data in staging area you transform it into dimension modeled data marts/ data warehouse. Staging layer holds data temporary when the data is loaded into data warehouse these records are deleted from stage.

Now let us see various ways of designing staging layer strategy.

While defining the strategy one have focus on:

1. What technique you will be using?
2. What kind of data load it will be, full data or incremental?
3. Where the staging data will reside?
4. Where aggregation will be performed?

There are following well-known techniques are available:

Data Storing Method

Data Stored First

In this technique, a data is stored in staging area and then used for transformation and loading into Data Warehouse environment

Data is first stored and then transformed if needed before forwarding

Direct Database insert/update

In this technique, a data is directly read from ODS and directly will be inserted or updated in the

Data read from source system and DML operation is done on DW with this selected data in the same transaction without any additional step

Data Warehouse environment

Data Gathering Method

Full Data

Here you use all the rows and update Data Warehouse environment with the data. This is time consuming process and the processing time will gradually increase because of data growth rate

> Full data load get all data records from the source system as an input and compare and load into DW

Delta or Incremental

Here you only get the changed/new records and you process these records so that information is passed to Data Warehouse environment

Types of Staging Data Stores:

> Delta only, process, changed or newly added records from source system

Data Storing Mode

File

Data can be placed in File. If more sorting operation needs to be performed then storing data in this format is beneficial

Table

Staging data can be stored in the table either permanently or for some time till it gets published to the Data Warehouse area

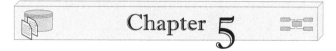

CHANGE DATA CAPTURE STRATEGY

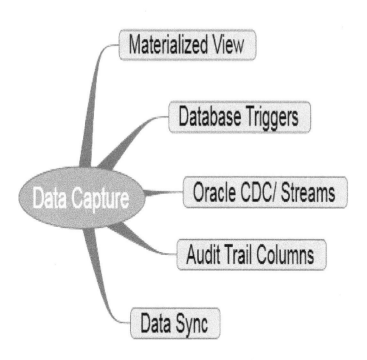

This chapter talks about all the possible ways to design change data capture methodology/strategy.

The options like Using Materialized view is explained in details along with other possible options.

In the Data warehousing project you need to pull the data from different environments.

There are various ways one can capture change data from the source. Let us see the various approaches in this chapter.

Materialized View

Another solution was using materialized view log. This log will be populated by the transaction log and can be used in materialized views. It is a three step process. First step was performed in the source database and other two were performed on the target database.

Step 1: Creating a Materialized Log in the source database

Create a materialized log on the desired table. A materialized view log must be in the source database in the same schema as the table. A table can have only one materialized view log defined on it.

There are two ways you can define this log, either on rowid or primary key. This log's name will be MLOG$_table_name which is an underlying table. This log can hold primary key, row ids, or object ids can also have other columns which will support a fast refresh option of materialized view which will be created based on this log.

When data changes are made to master table data, Oracle will pull these changes to the Materialized log as defined. The function of this log is to log the DML activities performed on the used table.

E.g. CREATE MATERIALIZED VIEW LOG ON table name WITH option like OBJECT ID, PRIMARY KEY or ROWID

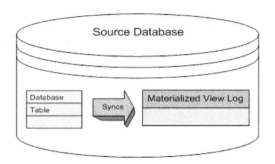

Figure 5.1 Step 1

Step 2: Creating a Materialized View in Target Database using this log

Create a Materialized view based on the above created materialized log. Materialized view is a replica of the desired table. This is like a table and needs to be refreshed periodically. You can define the needed refresh frequency to fast refresh this view based on the materialized log in the target database.

Whenever a DML operation is performed, on the defined table that activity will be recorded in the log which is in the Oracle 9i database, in the source system. Now we have a materialized view defined on this log in our system, Oracle 10g, which is target system. This view will only pull in the changes as defined in the log. These changes will be applied to the rows. One can define a desired frequency of refreshing this view. This process doesn't create any physical trigger, however there is a little overhead, as database has to store the row in the defined log table whenever a commit is issued.

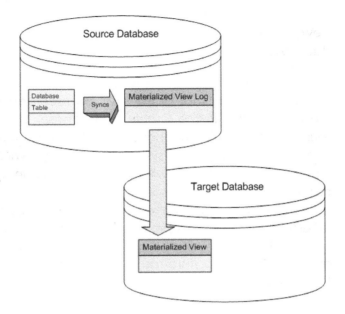

Figure 5.2 Step 2

Step 3: Creating a Change table

Now we will define a new table having same structure as of staging/source table with few additional columns.

The additional columns are, one for an indicator of which operation is done on the source table, e.g. INSERT, UPDATE, DELETE etc. One more column of numerical/ integer type to store the sequence of the operations. This is useful if you have more than one operation performed on the row, e.g., a new row is added so it is INSERT then the same row is modified so it is UPDATE. To have these two rows come in the sequence of the transaction this column can be useful.

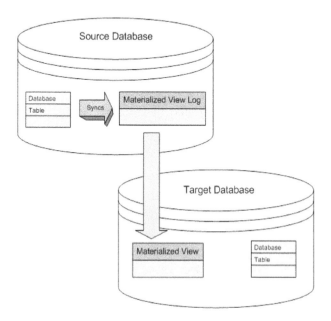

Figure 5.3 Step 3

Step 4: Writing triggers on Materialized View

As we know materialized views are like a table. We can have data base triggers on the table so we can use the same techniques for the newly create materialized view. In prior first two steps we saw how the changed data is pulled from the source system and will be loaded in the materialized view defined in the target system. Now the question is how to use this view to determine the changes. For this purpose we will write database triggers on this materialized view, triggers like after insert, after update and after delete.

These triggers will capture which operation was performed on the row then a record is inserted in the target change table to store the record with appropriate transaction mode and sequence number

Now whenever a DML operation is performed on the table, the log will get refreshed by the new information based on the defined frequency, then materialized view will be refreshed with the new information based on the information available in materialized log. Appropriate trigger will be fired based on the operation performed on the data row. This trigger will create a new record in the staging table with appropriate operation mode like: I for Insert, U for Update and D for Delete with the activity sequence number.

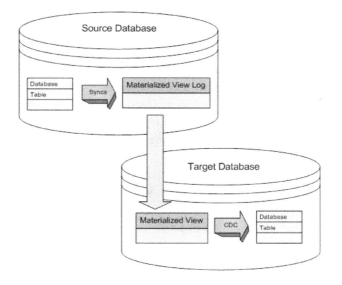

Figure 5,4 Step 4

Database Triggers

If you have a liberty of changing the source database you can use this approach. This will be adding some cost on the DML operations on the source database though. However this can be a feasible option in some cases where you cannot use any other option but want to have change data or delta data rather than full data.

Step1: Create a transaction or stage table

Create a transaction table which will hold the changes on the source table. You can create this transaction table in the source database or create a staging table in the stage environment which will hold the transactions of DML on the source table.

Step2: Create DML Triggers on source table

Create after insert/update/delete triggers on the source tables. These triggers will insert a record into a transaction table in source database or in staging table directly. This way we can capture the changes like update to the existing data or newly added data or deleted data. Whenever you implement it make sure to add a running number or surrogate key in the stage table which should be populated automatically like before insert trigger. This column can be used to get the sequence of data base transactions.

Audit Trail Columns

If the source table has audit trail columns and records data inserted date and data modified date you can use these audit trail columns to get the change data from the last successful data load job.

Data Sync

In Data Sync you compare the full data of source table with the data warehouse table and find out the difference which includes modified data records and newly inserted data records or deleted data records. Load these records in stage table to process it in data warehouse.

Oracle CDC or Streams

Oracle, have streams or CDC technology which can be used to capture changed data as well. This technology uses subscriber and publisher model. Use it to get the changed data into stage table directly and then process it further.

This page intentionally left blank

DATA WAREHOUSE STRATEGY

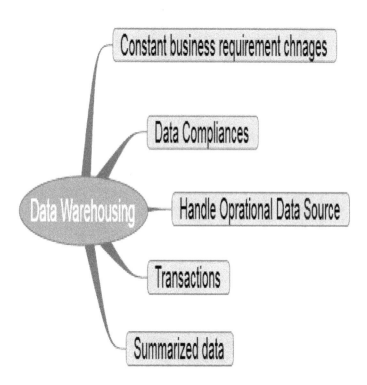

This chapter talks about new approach of building data warehouse which handles agile with data warehouse and many other small issues.

You need to consider various aspects while architecting data warehouse. Traditional data warehousing technique or approaches bring lot of things on the plate however now a day we are faced with some different challenges not just gathering or reorganizing data.

A new approach

We can follow either top down or bottom up approach to develop the data warehouse. While architecting we need to consider the issues like requirement changes constantly how we can design data warehouse which can accommodate changes easily. E.g. If we added one more column in the fact table we need to go back and update all the rows to have proper value in this column. This can be very costly based on the number of records in the fact table. How to handle this? How to have data warehouse and operational data source under one roof for better reporting? How to handle detailed level data and summarized data under one roof? How to have lifecycle, like Order lifecycle modeled? All these questions are handled in this new approach.

In traditional data warehousing we have to deal with dimension and facts. All the dimensions are of specific types, like Type1, Type2 or Type 3. In these dimensions you have number of attributes or columns related or describing the dimension.

Based on the type of the dimension the history is mentioned. Like in case of Type2 new records are added expiring the old ones or a last record data is updated in the row. During this process important point is to maintain the key id of dimension, so that the tie with fact will not be lost. In many cases we end up creating a running sequence id as a key and another id column as a dim key id.

In the dimension we still have other columns, even if we typed or categorized the dimension, all the attributes of this dimension may not follow the same categorization. In other words we may have a Type 2 dimension containing few columns which are of a type 1 and may also have some as a constant and will never change.

The overall technical architecture looks like in the diagram 6.1

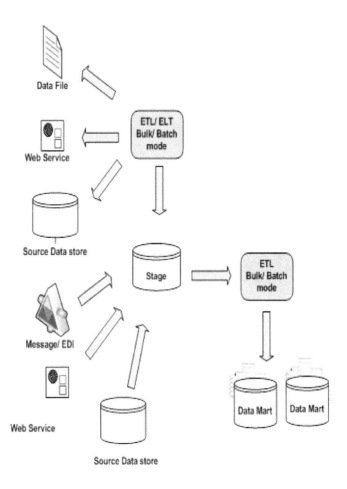

Figure 6.1 Approach

Let us see the different components of this approach.

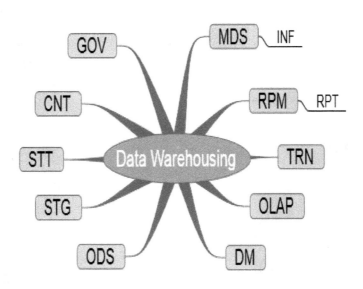

Figure 6.2 Mind map

STG tables:

STG stands for stage data source. This is the staging layer of your data warehouse. You can use the data staging strategy as explained before for designing this layer.

Create STG table for each source.

 STG have same data structure as of source table

Let us take an example and develop it along this different component to understand this topic little better.

Let us consider that we are building a data warehouse for order lifecycle tracking and revenue reporting kind of reports

For that we will create STG_sales_order, STG_Customer, STG_Product, STG_Channel

SEC tables:

SEC stands for security data source. This table will be used for security role integration with the data warehouse. This can be used for personalized dashboard kind of reporting.

We will create SEC_user_role table which will hold all the users have access to the data and their manager for rolling up the data

This table will be used in all the report or metadata joins for implementing personalized dashboard concept.

MDS tables:

MDS stands for master data source. MDS table is created based on constant value columns, like dim key id, source key reference id of that dimension, along with load id which is explained in job control section.

Now by creating this table we have eliminated the need of more than one ids in the dimension, we have also separated the dimension as if we are doing a vertical partitioning. Which brings many benefits like single version of that dimension, less data will be duplicated. If we are using traditional Type 2 case we will be adding the entire record even if just one column is changed.

This will save space, help creating single identity of the dimension through-out the data warehouse across the subject areas.

There will be only one MDS table for a given dimension, which mostly contains dim key and source reference key ids.

MDS tables are also beneficial for resolving or transforming the fact as it only contains three columns your queries are faster, as it contains less records your query hit is faster and thus it reduces your I/O and get you a faster id resolution which in turns gives a better ETL performance.

For our example we will create MDS_Customer, MDS_sales_order (as a dimension), MDS_product and MDS_Channel

INF tables:

INF stands for incremental fields. These are the attributes of a dimension which are not constant. These attributes may have some high frequency data with respect to changes and some are not that frequently changed. Some needs to preserve history some can be ok not to have history.

We can create separate INF tables in these cases. One INF which will have data with high change frequency for recoding history, one INF for other data element which are not that frequently changed may or may not need history.

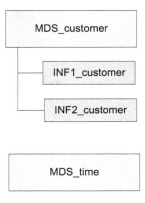

Figure 6.3 MDS

For our Example we will create INF1_customer to store all personal information of the customer then create INF2_customer to store other attributes which may or may not change overtime.

We will also create MDS_Time and MDS_Geography tables/dimensions.

RPM tables:

RPM stands for Reporting Master data source. This table contains ids of all the active records of MDS and INF tables to give end to end view of that dimension which is also helpful for lifecycle or status finding.

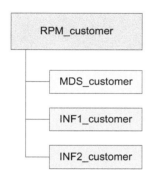

Figure 6.4 RPM

For our example we will have RPM_Customer for MDS_customer and INF1_customer and INF2_customer, similarly RPM_product for MDS_Product, INF1_product

TRN tables:

TRN stands for transaction data source. In traditional data warehousing we call it as a fact table. You can create one or more TRN tables for same fact. E.g. You have created a TRN table for order entered later you need to have more columns in the fact table for analytics you can create another TRN table for that instead of adding it in the same fact table like traditional approach.

TRN tables store the transformed data as it occurred which is good for historical reporting.

For our example we will create TRN_sales_order table, will transform and keep ids of all the required mds tables.

RPT tables:

RPT stands for master data source. In traditional data warehousing we have to deal with dimension and facts.

RPT table structure looks similar to TRN table however the data in RPT table is less compared to TRN table. RPT table only store the current picture of the data and does not store the history. This can be really helpful for reporting where you need to report on the as of picture and not required historical data.

This can be also helpful if you have lot of transaction changes and want to count or sum the transactions uniquely.

For our example we will create RPT_sales_order table

ODS tables:

ODS stands for operational data source. Now days we also need to combine the decision support reports with the enterprise report which are mostly result based report. In other words we need to combine data warehouse data with the real time data. This table can be utilized for that. All the needed table can be create in ODS layer and can be synced up with source using the data staging strategy as we worked on the data staging strategy chapter.

ODS tables will be in the same database or schema and can be linked to the MDS, INF tables using source_id column which is a reference key of the source which eventually a key of ODS table.

For our example we will create ODS_sales_order table

STT tables:

STT stands for status data source. To report on status or lifecycle we can use this table. This table will store all the status changes record and can be a part of RPM table along with respected MDS and INF tables. RPM table always will have the latest record id of STT table however if you want you can use this table for historical reporting.

For our example we will create STT_Sales_order which will records status like order entered, order prepared, order shipped, order invoiced, order return, order back order etc.

This page intentionally left blank

Chapter 7

DATA LOAD JOB
MANAGEMENT STRATEGY

Data_load_job_control
data_load_job_control_id
data_load_job_date
number_of_records_processed
number_of_records_inserted.....

Data_load_job_error
data_load_job_error_id
data_load_job_control_id
data_load_error_code
data_load_error_message......

This chapter talks about data load job management.

How it can be implemented and some design aspects to implement it.

Now that we saw the data staging strategy, change data capture strategy, information strategy and data warehouse strategy; let us see how we can manage all these data load jobs running in data warehouse.

Most of the industry standard tools come with a decent job management console. You can manage the jobs using that. Schedule a job to run or cancel a job; however they do not offer to rollback a particular job.

So this Data Load Job Management comes handy not just for PL/SQL or simpler ETL implementation however can be useful for any industry standard ETL tool as well.

Concept

In this strategy we will have to focus on questions like how we can rollback a particular job from all the tables. To do this let us introduce two tables, job control and job error.

Step1:

Create additional column in all the dimension and fact tables to hold a value of a data load job control id. Each data load job will be given an ID which will be recorded with the data in the target table.

Step 2:

Create "Data Load Job Control" table. This table will record all the meta-data about a job. Like run statistics, it status, like successful or failed or error, it records information like number of records processed number.

Data_load_job_control
data_load_job_control_id
data_load_job_date
number_of_records_processed
number_of_records_inserted......

Figure 7.1 Data Load Job Control table

Step 3:

Whenever a data load job started we will create an entry in the Job Control table and use the id for all the records inserted in the target tables.

Step 4:

Now in case you want to undone yesterday's job you can just find out the job control id from the job control table and use that id to delete the records from all data warehouse.

Error tracking:

Step 1: Create data Load job error table

A data load job error table can be created to record the error in a particular job. Error can be a database error which halted the load or can be balance and control error which will halt the further processing on this particular job.

Data_load_job_error
data_load_job_error_id
data_load_job_control_id
data_load_error_code
data_load_error_message……

Figure 7.2 Data Load Job Control table

Use this table in the error or exception tracking of your ETL code for tracking data base errors and in the code for tracking out of balance errors.

Thus any job lifecycle can be reported on using these two set of tables.

This page intentionally left blank

APPENDIX

Fastest way to compare in full data load

In the Data warehousing project you have dimension and fact tables. Usually, if data is coming from a single table, we can use the approach what I have presented in the last article "Change data capture for Oracle 9i database without adding triggers on the source table".

There are also plenty of other options available like CDC, using timestamp etc. However the problems come when you have a dimension table which is constructed based on a multi-table query. In this case none of the above approach can work directly.

Overview

Consider a case of Sales Representative dimension, this dimension is based several attributes like area, login etc. These attributes are coming from different tables. Now we will see what we can use to have an incremental update of this table.

The examples shown in this article is for Oracle database however same concept can be used for other database engines.

Step 1: Creating a Function which will return hash value

We will be using a hash value technique to compare the rows. Well we really have one more option, compare each field and see if any one of them is changed and that way determine the changed row.

However hash value method is faster than the above approach and code also become manageable with less conditional statements. Both methods are same though.

Create a function such that it will read a value as a text parameter and will return a hash value for it.

```
e.g.
FUNCTION salesrep_hashvalue (p_input_str
VARCHAR2)
RETURN VARCHAR2 IS
l_str VARCHAR2(20);
BEGIN
l_str := dbms_obfuscation_toolkit.md5(input_string =>
p_input_str);
```

RETURN l_str;
END salesrep_hashvalue;

Step 2: Add a new column in the dimension table to hold a hash value

Create a new column "hash value" in the dimension table. And update its value by using the above created function using the required columns.

Make sure you use the same set of columns and in the same sequence in the ETL logic to create a hash value for a new row.

Step 3: Write ETL code

In the ETL code read the records from this multi-table SQL in a cursor loop. For each record find out the hash key value. Gets the old hash key value by selecting the record from the dimension table using a key. If no records exist then insert the record. If record exists compare these tow hash keys if it is different update the record otherwise skip it.

Summary

This way you can achieve change data capture for a multi-table select statement query used for creation of a dimension table.

This page intentionally left blank

How to use Oracle's metadata package for impact analysis

Overview

Business is always changing and you have to make some changes based on the business requirement.

Before doing any change you want to perform an impact analysis. Most of the data modeling tools have provision to do it. I am focusing in the article how you perform this task if you don't have a tool.

Details

Consider a case, we have Oracle database and wants to alter a column width and would like to see wherever this column is used/ referenced. We can use Oracle's metadata package as indicated   below

```
SET pagesize 0

SET long 90000

SET feedback off

SET echo off
SELECT
DBMS_METADATA.GET_DDL('TABLE',ut.table_name)

FROM USER_TABLES ut;
```

This will give DDL scripts for all the tables. Now you can use any text tool like Notepad to search for the required column and find out the references.

Conclusion

There are various ways to do it. This is one of them. This will help you determining the impact exposure.

CDC Technique for dimension table which is based on a multi-table query

In the Data warehousing project you have dimension and fact tables. Usually, if data is coming from a single table, we can use the approach what I have presented in the last article "Change data capture for Oracle 9i database without adding triggers on the source table". There are also plenty of other options available like CDC, using timestamp etc. However the problem comes when you have a dimension table which is constructed based on a multi-table query. In this case none of the above approach can work directly.

Overview

Consider a case of Sales Representative dimension, this dimension is based several attributes like area, login etc. These attributes are coming from different tables. Now we will see what we can use to have an incremental update of this table. The examples shown in this article is for Oracle database however same concept can be used for other database engines.

Step 1: Creating a Function which will return hash value

We will be using a hash value technique to compare the rows. Well we really have one more option, compare each field and see if any one of them is changed and that way determine the changed row.

However hash value method is faster than the above approach and code also become manageable with less conditional statements. Both methods are same though. Create a function such that it will read a value as a text parameter and will return a hash value for it.

e.g.
```
FUNCTION dim_hashvalue (p_input_str VARCHAR2)
RETURN                 VARCHAR2              IS
l_str                           VARCHAR2(20);
BEGIN
l_str := dbms_obfuscation_toolkit.md5(input_string =>
p_input_str);
RETURN                                       l_str;
END                         dim_hashvalue;
```

Step 2: Add a new column in the dimension table to hold a hashvalue

Create a new column "hashvalue" in the dimension table. And update its value by using the above created function using the required columns.

Make sure you use the same set of columns and in the same sequence in the ETL logic to create a hash value for a new row.

Step 3: Write ETL code

In the ETL code read the records from this multi-table SQL in a cursor loop. For each record find out the hash key value. Gets the old hash key value by selecting the record from the dimension table using a key. If no record exists then insert the record. If record exists compare these tow hash keys if it is different update the record otherwise skip it.

Conclusion

This way you can achieve change data capture for a multi-table select statement query used for dimension table.

This page intentionally left blank

Another way to do data virtualization

Now let us see data virtualization and how we can practically do this. *Data virtualization* is getting lot of attention now-a-days. In current world business need of a data is changing. Previously Data warehouse used to support DSS applications and reporting tool like Dashboard and Scorecards which preliminary need summarized snapshot of a data.

However now the trend looks like going towards having a *mix of consolidated data and near-real time* data. There are few EII techniques and tools available for this however if you have to deliver this without spending a fortune you can leverage using database layer.

You can create a Data warehouse either top down or bottom up modeled and can have an ODS tables/schema to hold the ODS data without transformation. Various change data capture techniques can be used to keep ODS data in sync with the source, like in Oracle we can use Change data capture or Streams method.

Now since we are not transforming the ODS data it need to be transformed virtually. We can create a *view layer combining these two layers* to deliver data for some operational reporting and near real time data needs. Key is to transform the ODS data and fit it together with the data mart or data warehouse data.

There are two ways you can implement data virtualization in the data warehouse project. Let us consider two cases: first we have some kind of MPP environment and second non MPP environment.

Data Virtualization in MPP environment

Let me elaborate this term. By MPP I mean MPP architecture. Let us assume we have an Oracle database. We have implemented GRID on a RAC technology. To do this we need to create additional nodes. Data will be synchronized in these notes by database itself such that all these nodes will have same data.

This can follows no sharing architecture. All these nodes are practically separate schema so can be utilized separately if you want.

Let us assume we have four nodes in this RAC environment. We have developed our subject oriented data marts. Data coming into these marts is transformed from OLTP system to fit into dimensional model. Data has been gone through stage before. Some of the data elements passed through two stage layers before. These marts are refreshed nightly, taking the deltas from the source system.

You are implementing EII and according to it you want all the reporting to be done using data warehouse environment. We have nightly refreshed data from the data marts however we are lacking the today's data or current days' data. Most of the operational decision reporting needs current near real time data. So now we will have to implement data virtualization here.

Let us see how we can solve this. Since we have 4 nodes Oracle RAC, we can implement no sharing technique. To implement it we can create two different TNS settings, one to use first two nodes only and other to use another two nodes. Create a new user called "Reports" and make sure whenever the request is coming from this user it is always accessing node three and four. Please refer to the diagram.

Ok now we have OLTP data and data mart data. The task we have now if to combine this in such a way that it is faster for reporting. We already have designed data marts such a way that it will be faster for reporting using dimensional modeling however our ODS layer is relational modeled. We will have to create another virtual layer to combine these two layers. We can use Oracle views to do that with using synonyms and grants for required objects. We can also define a view to pull only today's data from the ODS and create a view to pull current or active data from data mart.

Then define another view which combined these two views. Now we have all the data needed in this virtual layer which can be used in business intelligence applications.

Data Virtualization in non-MPP environment

To attend data virtualization in non-MPP environment you can use the techniques explained in data warehouse strategy chapter.

ODS tables along with the data staging strategy with change data capture strategy that will deliver the changed data into this environment.

Performance Considerations

In the Data warehousing project you need to pull the data from different environments.

Design Technique for Date type columns

When you design a Data warehouse or Data Mart you come across many Date data type attributes in dimensions and/or facts tables. And. In this article I have pointed out a design technique for Date columns for fact table which gives highest performance.

Consider a data mart having a fact table "Order" with many columns like Order Number, Order Date, Shipped Date and Amount and a "Time" dimension which have an entry for each day. You use "timed" for "Order Date" however most of the time "Shipped Date" is kept as a Date column.

Consider in your reporting system you want to design a report to report number of orders shipped in a particular year. Now you will have format the shipped date column so that you can compare its year portion to get result. If you have a massive fact table this query is going to take more time as it will not be using any index, well you can create index to solve this problem.

Now consider you have a report which report number of orders shipped in a particular month, day, quarter etc. To speed up this operation you will have create index probably more than one. However if we use the id column and index on that column then you can avoid the above problem

Add shipped_date_id column along with the Shipped Date column in the fact table. Derive the value by using Time dimension. So whenever you query you always use index.

This way you can achieve maximum performance without adding more indexes. You can just go to your time dimension get the required ids and join it with your fact table which will use index defined on "shipped_date_id" column.

To get more scalable performance we can leverage parallel processing of a query to do that we can define partitions on the target table and move data and index to these partitions which will reduce the overall I/O read.

Design Technique for Fact tables

Fact table can also be partitions based on the need, like range partitions of date/year.

Design Technique for Dimension tables

Multiple partitions can be created, on same file server or different based on the need and then allocated for different partitions.

This page intentionally left blank

INDEX

This page intentionally left blank

About the Author

Milind has completed MS in computer science and Management and have been working in IS around past 13 years. Have worked on various area and have specialized in data warehouse and business intelligence solutions and currently working as an Enterprise Data Architect.

This page intentionally left blank

www.ingramcontent.com/pod-product-compliance
Lightning Source LLC
Chambersburg PA
CBHW052148070326
40689CB00050B/2522